The Livonian Brothers of the Sword: The History of the Medieval Catholic Military Order that Fought Pagans in Eastern Europe

By Charles River Editors

The seal

About Charles River Editors

Charles River Editors is a boutique digital publishing company, specializing in bringing history back to life with educational and engaging books on a wide range of topics. Keep up to date with our new and free offerings with this 5 second sign up on our weekly mailing list, and visit Our Kindle Author Page to see other recently published Kindle titles.

We make these books for you and always want to know our readers' opinions, so we encourage you to leave reviews and look forward to publishing new and exciting titles each week.

Introduction

The coat of arms

    For centuries, Christians and Muslims were embroiled in one of the most infamous territorial disputes of all time, viciously and relentlessly battling one another for the Holy Land. In the heart of Jerusalem sat one of the shining jewels of the Christian faith, the Church of the Holy Sepulchre. Legend has it that this was where their Savior had been buried before his fabled resurrection. What was more, it was said to house the very cross Jesus Christ had died upon. It was for precisely these reasons that fearless pilgrims, near and far, risked their lives and made the treacherous trek to Jerusalem.

    Like other secretive groups, the mystery surrounding the Catholic military orders that sprung up in the wake of the First Crusade helped their legacies endure. While some conspiracy theorists attempt to tie the groups to other alleged secret socities like the Illuminati, other groups have tried to assert connections with them to bolster their own credentials. Who they were and what they had in their possession continue to be a source of great intrigue.

    Although many have heard of the Crusades and some of the more famous orders like the Templars, few know about the Livonian Crusade or the Livonian Brothers of the Sword. This organization was one of many Catholic military orders that sprung up during the Middle Ages in response to the papacy's call for holy war, and the Livonian Crusade is the term used to group together dozens of military actions undertaken by German knights in Eastern Europe.

In essence, the Holy Roman Empire sought to control influential trade routes throughout the region by subjugating the native peoples and forcefully converting them to Christianity, and in this regard, the differences between the Livonian Crusade and those taking place further east, where crusaders attempted to retake the Christian Holy Land of Jerusalem, are readily apparent. In particular, there was no actual religious justification for the Livonian Crusade, and many of the knights deciding to join were often more interested in the political and economic benefits gained from the war. When it comes to understanding the history of the Livonian Brothers of the Sword, scholars have their work cut out for them, as few primary sources survived the conflict, and the order has had many different names over the years, including the Swordbrothers, the Livonian Order, and the Swordbrothers.

All that said, the Livonian Brothers of the Sword bore many similarities to their counterparts in other countries, including being affiliated with the Catholic Church. Many of the knights took vows of celibacy and poverty, and the internal structure of the organization could be compared to the Knights Hospitaller or the Templars. Moreover, while relatively few people know of the Livonian Brothers of the Sword by their original name, the order would go on to become one of the most influential of religious knighthoods by incorporating into the Teutonic Knights. The order was also significant for consolidating the power of the Holy Roman Empire in Eastern Europe, as well as subjugating the native peoples and spreading Christianity by force, leading to numerous tensions that lasted centuries between the future nations of Estonia, Prussia, and others.

The Livonian Brothers of the Sword: The History of the Medieval Catholic Military Order that Fought Pagans in Eastern Europe chronicles the known history of the order and examines the important battles the order fought in. Along with pictures of important people, places, and events, you will learn about the Livonian Brothers of the Sword like never before.

The Livonian Brothers of the Sword: The History of the Medieval Catholic Military Order that Fought Pagans in Eastern Europe

About Charles River Editors

Introduction

    The Crusades and the Birth of Knighthood

    The Origins of the Livonian Brothers

    Fighting the Estonians

    Fighting Saaremaa

    Fighting the Semigallians

    The Fall of the Teutonic Knights

    The Livonian Chronicle of Henry

    The Structure of the Order

    The Influence of the Knights in Nationalism and Popular Culture

    Online Resources

    Bibliography

Free Books by Charles River Editors

Discounted Books by Charles River Editors

The Crusades and the Birth of Knighthood

"You are called shepherds; see that you do not act as hirelings. But be true shepherds, with your crooks always in your hands. Do not go to sleep, but guard on all sides the flock committed to you...For according to the gospel, you are the salt of the earth. But if you fall short in your duty, how, it may be asked, can it be salted?" – Pope Urban II

The silky sea of sand dunes seems to stretch endlessly, the grains appearing almost golden under the glow of the scorching midday sun. A swirl of sand dances daintily across the open space as a gust of wind blows past. The scenery would have been stunning, if it were not for the swarm of black figures from afar, steadily gaining in size. The ground quakes from the pounding hooves of a thousand horses, the iron-clad men mounted on top of them brandishing their weapons and shields. Even from a distance, their thunderous cries rumble across the open space, their words as clear as the day was: "Kill all the infidels!"

Charging from the opposite side is an equally formidable sight. Hundreds upon hundreds of men in glinting armor lean forward with their reins clutched between their fists, the quilted coverings on their dressed stallions rippling behind them. Alongside them are countless men sporting turbans and conical helmets, wielding bows and arrows, spears, and mighty swords.

This is often what springs to mind when the crusades are brought into conversation, but not only are the roots of these wars far more complex and its barbarism often glorified in modern pop culture, it spawned generations of legendary chivalric orders.

For starters, a "crusade" was a holy war, but for them to be classified as such, they had to be approved by the pope. These papal-endorsed military campaigns aimed on squashing the so-called Islamic "infidels" and enemies of Christ. But while it might appear as if the Catholics were only concerned with takeovers and forced conversions, there was far more going on under the hood than meets the eye.

Following centuries of persecution, Christianity became the official religion of the Roman Empire under Constantine the Great, and the eastern half of the Empire (which later became the Byzantine Empire) took charge of Jerusalem and the Levant, controlling the area and its flow of pilgrims. But after the collapse of Rome, the Byzantines were displaced in the early 7th century by a third "Abrahamic" (after the semi-legendary founder of Judaism, Abraham) religion known as Islam, which came out of the Arabian Peninsula. An Arab Muslim army took Jerusalem in 634 A.D., and with that the Holy Land was lost to the Christians, who mourned its loss for centuries as they remained unable to take it back.

This sense of loss was exacerbated by disputes over pilgrimage rights to Jerusalem for both Christians and Jews. Since attitudes from one Muslim ruler to the next were fluid in regard to tolerance of minority religious groups, this added to a sense of uncertainty regarding Christian and Muslim access to the holy shrines, access which was paramount to ongoing Christian and Jewish identity. While it remains unclear how tolerant Muslim attitudes in the Levant during this time were over the long-term, the lack of control of such holy sites contributed to a sense of permanent anxiety among the Christians especially. Continuing patterns of expansion and contraction on the borders of the Byzantine Empire also added to the political instability of the region.

However, in the 11th century, the Arab Muslims also lost control of the Levant to a new group coming in from West Asia through Persia and Anatolia – the Seljuq Turks. After being brought in as mercenaries in 1058, they gained control of the Abassid dynasty in Baghdad, taking most of Anatolia from the failing Byzantine Empire and also conquering most of the Levant. This was part of their original purpose of fighting the new Fatimid dynasty in Egypt.

Even at its height, the Seljuq Empire lacked a strong infrastructure and existed in a state of perpetual warfare. Syria, in the Western Levant, was loosely organized into squabbling leaders distantly swearing allegiance to Baghdad and soon began to fall apart, while Palestine was contested by the Fatimids. In the wake of the empire's growing weakness, the Byzantine Emperor, Alexius Comnenus (1056-1118), saw an opportunity to regain some territory. He had hired Frankish mercenaries before, so he sent a letter to the Pope in Rome asking for more help. What was different was the Pope's reaction, which was quite startling. He called for something new – a crusade.

It is also not entirely clear how Pope Urban II came up with the idea of a crusade to the Holy Land. Gregory had made a previous call in 1074, using the term, "*milites Christi*" (soldiers of Christ), but it had been largely ignored. It is possible that Urban had heard of the Muslim concept of jihad or holy war, and the concept of aggressive expansion through holy war was not at all unknown to Christians by that period. However he conceived the idea, Urban decided to give a speech calling his audience to go on a crusade to the Holy Land, to win back Jerusalem and cleanse the Holy Land of the Muslim threat, using the Byzantine Emperor's letter as an excuse.

It is unlikely that he was aware that he would get the response that he did, for it was unprecedented. He had perhaps hoped at best to gain some mercenaries to send to the Emperor, a few donations, even an small army. With that said, his speech was not spontaneous; he had planned it very carefully, maneuvering to bring in leaders of the crusade before announcing it.

Urban spoke to a large number of people in Clermont, France on November 27, 1095. This was known as the Council of Clermont, and the subject was the letter from Alexius. After a brief exhortation against the fratricidal violence of the knights (Urban, himself, came from nobility), Urban related the news that the Seljuqs had conquered Romania and were attacking Europe as far west as Greece. He painted a picture of Christianity in grave danger from this new, Turkish threat, even mentioning them separately from the Arabs as another group of enemies against

Christians in the Middle East.

The actual text of Urban's speech does not survive, but some chroniclers related the general tenor and structure of it, and there were no less than five accounts from possible eyewitnesses, as well as relatively fanciful and elaborate reconstructions from a generation later, such as Fulcher of Chartres' (c.1059-1127) *History of the Expedition to Jerusalem*, which was written about 30 years later. Even those completed relatively close to the time were written after the fall of Jerusalem to the crusaders. Baldric of Dol's (c.1050-1130) *Historiae Hierosolymitanae libri IV*, Guibert of Nogent's (c.1055-1124) *Dei gesta per Francos* ("God's deeds through the Franks"), Robert the Monk's (d. 1122) *Historia Hierosolymitana*, Fulcher of Chartres' chronicle, and the anonymously written *Gesta Francorum* (Deeds of the Franks) comprise the main primary sources for the crusade.

Depiction of Pope Urban II preaching the First Crusade at the Council of Clermont.

According to Fulcher of Chartres, the pope said, "I, or rather the Lord, beseech you as Christ's heralds to publish this everywhere and to pers-e all people of whatever rank, foot-soldiers and knights, poor and rich, to carry aid promptly to those Christians and to destroy that vile race from the lands of our friends. I say this to those who are present, it is meant also for those who are absent. Moreover, Christ commands it." Fulcher of Chartres has Urban II continue:

"All who die by the way, whether by land or by sea, or in battle against the pagans, shall have immediate remission of sins. This I grant them through the power of God with which I am invested. O what a disgrace if such a despised and base race, which worships demons, should conquer a people which has the faith of omnipotent God and is made glorious with the name of Christ! With what reproaches will the Lord overwhelm us if you do not aid those who, with us, profess the Christian religion! Let those who have been accustomed unjustly to wage private warfare against the faithful now go against the infidels and end with victory this war which should have been begun long ago. Let those who for a long time, have been robbers, now become knights. Let those who have been fighting against their brothers and relatives now fight in a proper way against the barbarians. Let those who have been serving as mercenaries for small pay now obtain the eternal reward. Let those who have been wearing themselves out in both body and soul now work for a double honor. Behold! on this side will be the sorrowful and poor, on that, the rich; on this side, the enemies of the Lord, on that, his friends. Let those who go not put off the journey, but rent their lands and collect money for their expenses; and as soon as winter is over and spring comes, let them eagerly set out on the way with God as their guide."

Depiction of Pope Urban II

The campaign attracted thousands of hopefuls, each bearing their own agendas. The warrior class was primed and ready to fight, for that was their bread and butter, and the crusade presented them with a rare type of freedom they were not about to pass on. Their violence was not only sanctioned by the Church, they needed not be restricted by their usual employers, nor did they have to risk losing any of their territories.

The Church, recently reorganized and instilled with a new fire by the Gregorian Reform led by one of Urban's predecessors, Gregory VII, was just as ready to rise to the challenge. European Christians were taught – or brainwashed, depending on how one approaches it – to display total intolerance to heathens exhibiting "irreligious behavior." Many believed it their mission to guide these heathens to the light of God at all costs, even if it meant breaking the commandments, which in this case, they believed to be for the greater good.

Feudal Europe implemented what was known as the "primogeniture" system, wherein the firstborn sons automatically inherited the patriarch's titles and lands. This might have paved a solid path for the futures of the eldest sons in European families, but unless these firstborns were struck down by the plague or some other ill force of nature, this system left the second sons and so forth with no choice but to seek alternative venues for survival. Enterprising minds founded their own businesses and found other ways to make money, but many became hired guns, mercenaries, and the very first knights. These were the same men who were said to have made up the bulk of the crusaders.

Other reasons for enlistment were many and varied. Younger sons hoped to try their luck at conquering new lands and obtaining new properties overseas that they could call their own. Some seized the opportunity to broaden their horizons, and though this might have not been the ideal way to do it, sailing across the seas for an adventure was a motivation that sufficed for many. Kings rounded up rogue and ungovernable knights who needed an outlet for their bloodlust, and thereby rerouted their kleptomaniac itches towards enemy troops and villagers.

To medieval folks, salvation was measured by a figurative balance scale of sorts. One side weighed one's righteous acts, and the other, one's evil deeds; whichever side bore more weight indicated the salvation or damnation of one's soul. With that in mind, it was the Catholic mentality that all it took for a ticket to heaven was to even the score. This meant that racking up "righteous acts," including journeying on pilgrimages and obeying papal orders, could add the weight needed for the entry to Heaven. As a result, many sinners, particularly knights and warriors who had taken many a life, were some of the first to queue up for the enlistment. After all, Urban had assured them, "All who die by the way, whether by land or by sea, or in battle against the [Muslims], shall have immediate [forgiveness] of sins."

These knights who would fight for the cause came from all walks of life, and to cement their undying loyalty to the Christian faith, a cross was emblazoned across each and every one of their chests.

A year after Urban's famous speech, 4 armies of crusaders, each spearheaded by a different European power, prepped themselves to set sail for the Byzantine territories, and scheduled the date of departure for August of 1096. In an effort to seek glory for themselves, the overeager and much less experienced army of Peter the Hermit, who christened themselves the "People's Crusade," left about a month or two before the rest of the crusaders, defying the advice of Alexios himself. When Peter's army arrived at their destination, they were greeted by the far more seasoned Muslim troops, and put out of their misery in Cibotus. Soon after came the crusaders of Count Emicho, who proceeded to wreak unchecked havoc across the Jewish communities of Rhineland. To Urban's dismay, the disobedience of Emicho, which led to the slaughter of hundreds of innocent Jews, strained Christian-Jewish relations, which was not part of the plan.

The disastrous consequences of Peter and Emicho's insubordination was precisely why each of the 4 crusader armies were made to pledge an oath of loyalty to the pope, to which all 3, apart from Bohemond of Taranto's forces, complied. The delay proved to be worthwhile, for in May of 1097, the crusaders stormed into Nicea, the Seljuk capital of Anatolia, and had their flags planted by the end of June. One year later, the Syrian city of Antioch was theirs.

Inspired by their string of successes, the crusaders decided it was time for the main event, and headed for Jerusalem. There, they faced off with the troops of the Shi'ite Islamic caliphate, better known as the "Egyptian Fatimids." Halfway through July of 1099, the locals caved, and to the delight of the crusaders, Jerusalem was theirs once more, closing the curtains on the First Crusade. Be that as it may, Tancred, Bohemond's nephew, had given his word to the Muslim leaders that the locals would be spared. Sadly, hundreds of innocents, including children, had fallen victim to the crusaders' swords by the end of the ordeal, which left an even fouler taste in Muslim mouths.

Medieval depiction of the Siege of Jerusalem

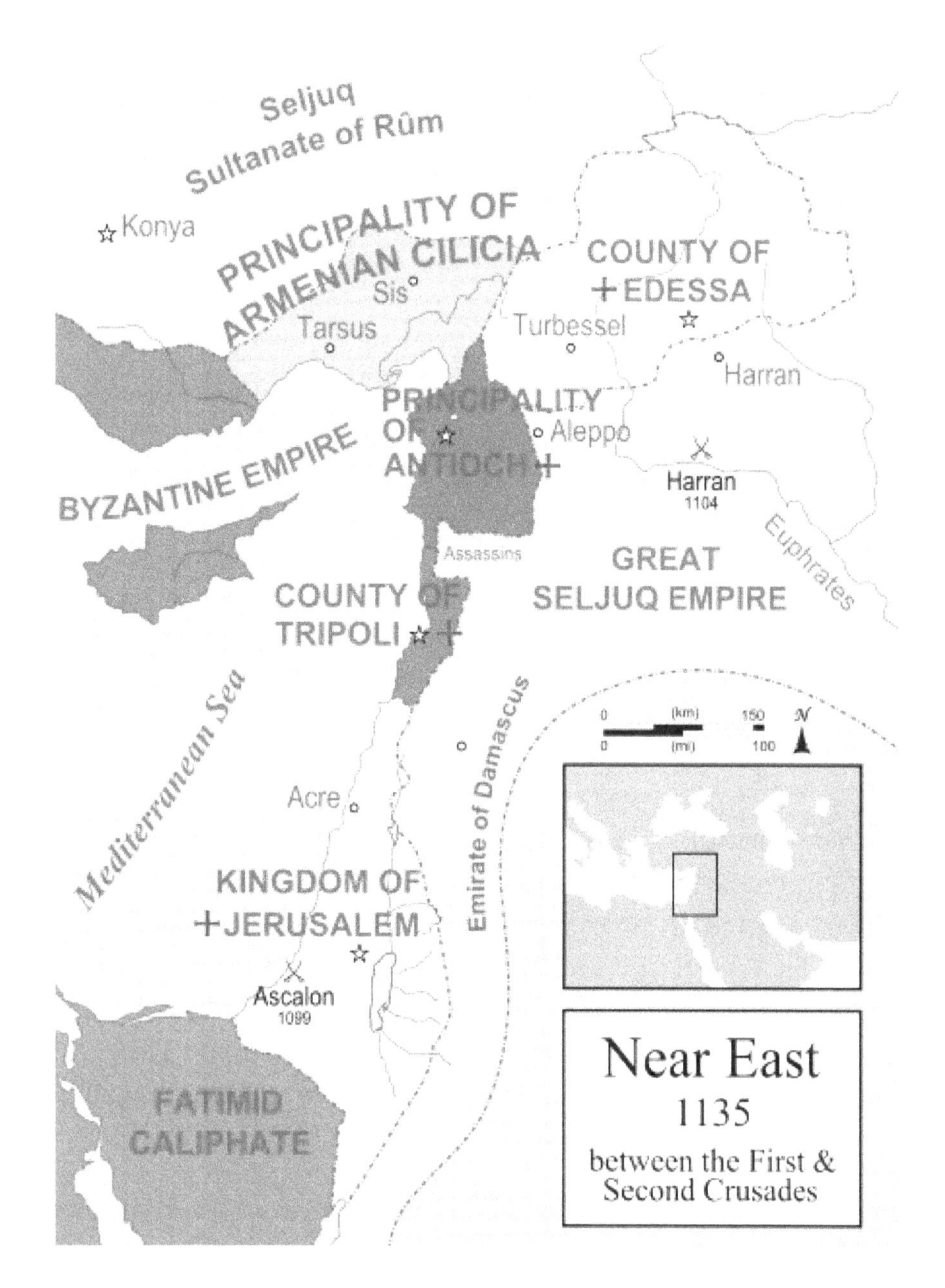

The Crusader States

    Contrary to modern Muslim views of the Crusades, contemporary Islam was not especially traumatized or disrupted by the Crusades. The First Crusade in particular had little effect on the Muslim chroniclers, and the Muslim response is found scattered through various histories of what their writers considered greater concerns.

    There were various reasons for this. First, Palestine existed in a contested area between the Abbasid Seljuq Empire of Baghdad in what is now Iraq and the Fatimid Empire in Egypt, based in Cairo. The contemporary and even later Muslim sources seemed to be confused about the origins and intent of the Crusaders. Further, both empires were not cohesive entities but squabbling groups of city rulers that existed in a fragile and constantly shifting set of alliances and rivalries. There was very little consistency of Muslim loyalty or alliance and no Pan-Arab, let alone Pan-Muslim, identity. Ibn Al-Athir, for example, believed that the Franks had been hired as mercenaries by the Fatimids against the Abbasids, not by the Byzantines to reclaim Byzantine territory. The religious motive of crusade was largely ignored.

Another important reason the First Crusade was probably downplayed by Muslim writers was the fact that the chroniclers were mostly Arabs, but most of the armies that the Crusaders fought were Turkish armies fighting for Turkish interests. The Seljuqs had recently displaced the Arab elites, so there was a disconnect between the damage the Crusaders were doing to individual rulers and the concerns of the writers recording the events. Unlike the Frankish, or even the Byzantine source of Anna Comnena, the Arab historians felt little personal involvement in the events surrounding the crusade and thus did not ascribe great importance to it.

Lastly, and perhaps most importantly, the Crusaders did not threaten the actual centers of Muslim power by passing through and claiming the contested territory of Palestine and western Syria. The distant power centers of Baghdad and Cairo were never touched or threatened, so the Crusaders were not considered a great threat by either the Abbasid Sultan or the Fatimid Caliph. This attitude would change, but not for several decades.

Meanwhile, as they were still riding the high of a victory that came much sooner than expected, many of the crusaders made the journey back home. A fraction was left behind to manage the newly conquered territories, which they called "Crusader States," or by its alternative moniker, the "Outremer," a take on the French translation of "overseas." The 4 Crusader States consisted of dominions in Jerusalem, Antioch, Tripoli, and Edessa, where new Christian-governed castles and fortifications would rise from the ashes. Their rule was uninterrupted for about 45 years, until Zangi, the general of Mosul, and his men broke through the borders of Edessa unannounced and seized the state in 1144.

The loss of Edessa bruised the egos of the European Christian leaders back home, and 3 years later, Pope Eugene III called for a Second Crusade. These would be the first of the campaigns to be directed by monarchs – the German King Conrad III and the French King Louis VII. Hoping to score more victories, the crusaders under Conrad marched into Dorylaeum, where they had emerged triumphant during the First Crusade. Conrad and Louis then consolidated their forces at Jerusalem and set forth for the Syrian-owned Damascus with an army upwards of 50,000.

As impressive as the crusader armies were, they were no match for the Turkish forces, who had called upon Zangi's successor, Nur al-Din, for added reinforcement. By 1149, the crusaders were crushed and driven out of Damascus, abruptly concluding the Second Crusade. 5 years later, authority of Damascus was passed on to the leader of Mosul.

The wounds that came with the defeat of the crusaders were reopened in 1187. In early July that year, Saladin (the sultan of Egypt and the creator of the Ayyubid Dynasty) and his troops crossed the River Jordan and touched ground in the Kingdom of Jerusalem. Among Saladin's first orders of business was to lay siege to the fortress in Tiberias. Back in the base of the crusaders, leaders convened to brainstorm tactics that would overwhelm the growing threat of Saladin and his forces. In spite of their enormous army, the crusaders' erroneous calculations had them walking straight into the Saladin's trap.

To suppress Saladin's men in Tiberias, the crusaders had to make an excruciating trek of over 12 miles, a task made all the more difficult due to their lack of water, limited supplies, and the sweltering heat beating down on their backs. The crusaders decided to make a stopover and made it to Hattin, but just barely. There, the alarmed crusaders found that Saladin's forces had already beat them to the punch, and were standing guard over the only fresh water source, the Sea of Galilee. Saladin's men launched an ambush on the haggard crusaders, and by the end of the chaos, now immortalized as the "Battle of Hattin," almost all of the crusaders were decimated, or shackled and claimed as prisoners of war. Among the captured was Guy of Lusignan, the king of the now crumbled crusader state of Jerusalem.

For the next 2 months, Saladin resumed his quest to capture more territories by the Levantine coast, and soon, added Acre, Nablus, Sidon, Jaffa, Toron, Ascalon, and Beirut to his expanding empire. In September of 1187, Saladin set his sights on the grand prize, and guided his troops towards the gates of Jerusalem. Following a vicious battle that lasted 10 days incited by crusaders making a last-ditch attempt to quell the invaders, Bailan of Ibelin, who had been placed in command in the king's absence, raised his white flag. As of October 4, 1187, Jerusalem was yet again under Muslim possession.

With tensions brought forth by the ongoing tug-of-war between Muslim and Christian powers at an all-time high, it was more crucial than ever to revamp the Outremer armies, and men from even more diverse backgrounds volunteered to pitch in to help the cause. The main class consisted of the knights and their tenants-in-chief, which were barons, bishops, and abbots. In this case, the knights in question referred not just to armored men on horses, but fighting units composing of individual soldiers on horseback, and their squires, which were knights-in-training that served their superiors. Vassal knights were those who were given land in exchange for their military service, while "retained" or "household knights," as previously mentioned, were landless men who were compensated with yearly salaries. These salaries could be cashed or converted to food, clothing, horses, and other valuable supplies.

Another component to the backbone of the Outremer armies were pilgrims either reeled in by religious fast-talkers – particularly during "Pilgrim Season" between the months of April and October – or those moved by the cause. Count Philip of Flanders, who barged into Acre in 1177, was one of the top pilgrim recruiters. His army there included several earls from Meath, Essex, and other high-ranking members of the English upper class.

Mercenaries and other experts on the battlefield were hired in droves to fill in where well-meaning, but untrained farmers could not. These trained men were needed to operate crossbows and other advanced weapons, as well as to lead what would otherwise have been a band of directionless farmers in suits of armor. Many of these farmers were serfs, servants, and indentured laborers that were promised their freedom, should they join the crusade. Then, there were the Turcopoles, a name given to Christian converts of Arabic descent. Tucopoles were free men from other crusader states who bore grudges against the Turks for heavy taxes and other injustices, or those made to serve under the "Arriere Ban" by the King of Jerusalem.

Last, but not least, there were the fighting monks. These militant orders were founded with the sole mission to defend Jerusalem and its Christian pilgrims, and among these fabled chivalric orders, the Livonian Brothers of the Sword would sprout up.

The Origins of the Livonian Brothers

The Livonian Brothers of the Sword did not participate in any fighting near Jerusalem, but the organization was founded shortly after the papacy called for the First Crusade. While the Crusades are now almost completely associated with the conflicts fought against Muslims to the east, they encompassed other areas as a series of religious wars sanctioned by the Catholic Church against enemies deemed heretical due to their devotion to different gods or failure to uphold the tenets and theology of the Latin institution. A crusade could be called to stamp out Paganism, for example, as with the Livonian Brothers of the Sword in Eastern Europe. The primary targets of the Crusades were Jerusalem in the Middle East and the Eastern Mediterranean, which was threatened by the Islamic Caliphates and the growing Ottoman Empire. It should also be noted that while current historians refer to these holy wars as the Crusades, this term was not popularized until 1760. Contemporary medieval people referred to the actions of the Catholic Church as the religious or holy wars.

The First Crusade established numerous precedents for future holy wars. In particular, pilgrims and crusaders would come from all classes to take public vows and receive plenary indulgences from the Church. Many participants hoped there would be a mass ascension of the faithful to heaven from Jerusalem, and this morphed into the Catholic Church's granting indulgences guaranteeing God's forgiveness for an individual's sins, which became a major draw for nobles and soldiers who worried about the consequences of their plundering and murdering during warfare. Other people joined the Crusades to obtain glory, raise their social status, gain political power, and satisfy obligations to feudal lords, and many of these elements would also ring true for those in the Livonian Brothers of the Sword.

Despite the initial success, the Crusades would ultimately fail, but while the last Catholic outposts in the Middle East fell by the end of the 13th century, outposts continued to exist in Northern and Western Europe, where the enemies were not Muslims and Turks but peoples viewed as pagan and heretical to the Catholic Church. The Wendish Crusade resulted in the groups living in the Northeast Baltic felling under Catholic control, strengthening Central

Europe, and in the early 13th century, the Teutonic Order would develop a new Crusader state in Prussia, creating a holy order that defended and controlled much of the Baltic region. The French monarchy also extended its empire through the Albigensian Crusade, which brought French territory straight to the Mediterranean Sea. By 1492, the Christian kingdoms of the Iberian Peninsula managed to throw out the Moors, who had controlled part of the land for over 700 years. That happened to be the same year Columbus sailed east and ended up in the Americas, and from there, interests in conquest moved away from the Mediterranean and across the Atlantic Ocean to the New World.

A map of the Baltic circa 1200

Meanwhile, the Livonian Brothers of the Sword plied Christianity on the eastern shores of the Baltic Sea, primarily in Livonia but also in many other small counties and kingdoms making up the region. Today, the Baltic Sea is enclosed by modern Denmark, Estonia, Finland, Latvia, Lithuania, Sweden, northeast Germany, Poland, Russia, and the North and Central European Plain, and the Livonian Brothers of the Sword's main enemies were native Baltic peoples populating the region and forming small counties of ethnically and culturally similar groups.

Ironically, the first foe was the Livonians themselves, who lived close to the north coast of the Baltic Sea and stood in the way of profitable German trade routes. Other enemies living further to the south included the Estonians, Latgalians, Semigallians, Selonians, Curonians, Lithuanians, Skalvians, and Prussians. Over time, as the order grew more powerful, the Livonian Brothers of the Sword would count many native individuals among their allies, especially as regional tensions compelled various indigenous groups to side with the invading Germans in hopes of settling scores and gaining long-desired territory.

The presence of profitable trade routes was the primary reason behind the Catholic Church's desire for control over Eastern Europe. This gave the creation of the Livonian Brothers of the Sword a financial aspect, as many of the knights sought wealth and glory rather than the actual spread of Christianity. Centuries later, Enlightenment thinkers who harbored a healthy skepticism of the Church would note such motivations, and after Voltaire ruefully described the Holy Roman Empire as "neither holy nor Roman nor an empire," the adage has clung to the empire ever since.[1]

However, by the time Voltaire made that observation, the Holy Roman Empire had planted roots in Central Europe nearly 1,000 years earlier, and during the Livonian Brothers of the Sword's existence, the Holy Roman Empire was holy and an empire, albeit no longer Roman in culture or economy. In fact, the Holy Roman Empire was a multiethnic network of territories and provinces throughout Western and Central Europe established in the Early Middle Ages, and it would eventually spread to Eastern Europe and continue to be an influential power until its dissolution in 1806 at the hands of Napoleon.

The largest territory controlled by the empire was the Kingdom of Germany, from which many of the Livonian Brothers of the Sword hailed. Other significant territories included the Kingdom of Bohemia, the Kingdom of Burgundy, and the Kingdom of Italy, which included much of the land near Rome. As such, the empire wielded influence throughout Europe and controlled numerous trade routes, including ones that went through Eastern Europe's pagan lands.

The Vatican crowned the emperor of the Holy Roman Empire and in theory wielded almost absolute power throughout the territories, although he relied upon the local princes to keep the peace. Thus, even as multiple rulers tried to consolidate power on the throne, the empire functioned like a massive bureaucracy rooted in feudalism, giving the knights who joined the Livonian Brothers of the Sword opportunities to carve out spheres of power and influence for themselves.

The Livonian Brothers of the Sword could be considered a Teutonic religious knighthood, and it was established by the third bishop of Riga in 1202. Pope Innocent III sanctioned the establishment of the new order again in 1204, giving the Livonian Brothers more legitimacy. At

---

[1] Voltaire 1756

this time, the majority of the order's membership was comprised of German warrior monks who had gathered to battle nearby Finnic and Baltic pagans inhabiting Latvia, Lithuania, and Estonia. They were thus an Eastern European order, although many of the knights hailed from Central Europe and moved east in an attempt to spread Christianity and the burgeoning power of the Church.

A medieval depiction of Pope Innocent III

An illustration of a Teutonic Knight on the left and a Swordbrother on the right

The Livonian Crusade led by the order actually began in 1198, four years before the organization was granted legitimacy, and this crusade distinguished itself from other contemporary crusades because "the expeditions which went to Livonia were not accompanied by a papal legate," a standard feature in other holy wars declared by the Catholic Church.2 It also started with a war against the Livonians and Latgalians rather than an initial conflict between Christians and "heretics." Christianity had arrived in Latvia around the 7th century when a group of Swedish settlers built the town of Grobiņa, and its presence was reinforced by the Danes in the 11th century when settlers moved to the area. Christianity, however, was limited to foreign settlements, so many natives continued to practice their original religions.

This would be the situation into which Germans stumbled in the second half of the 12th century when they began trading along one of the most ancient Greek routes, stretching across Varangian territory. Only a small fraction of the indigenous population was baptized, and even fewer adhered to the tenets of the Church.

In 1184, a man named Saint Meinhard of Segeberg made it his mission to convert native Livonians to Christianity. He arrived in the town of Ikšķile and received permission for his work

---

[2] Brundage 1972:4

from the Bishop of Uxkull in 1186, and this small settlement was the central driving force of all missionary activities in Livonia in the late 12th century, making it the perfect starting place for Meinhard.

Conversations came easily at first. Native Livonians had lost to the nearby East Slavic Principality of Polotsk and were forced to pay tribute. They were also under attack from the Semigallians to the south and needed allies fast. Thus, when Low Germans like Meinhard, called Saxons, arrived, they seemed like the best choice. The Saxons exerted some influence and clearly had power since they were able to maintain a settlement despite its being in unfriendly territory.

Around 1189, a Livonian leader named Caupo of Turaido would be the first prominent individual to convert, undergoing a full baptism, but few conversions followed. While the local Livonians seemed interested in being baptized, they did not want to adhere to the rules Christianity placed on its followers. Nonetheless, the Livonians helped the missionaries maintain their settlement in exchange for trade and resources for a few years.

The situation grew rapidly dire in 1193, when Pope Celestine III called for a crusade against all pagans in Northern Europe, including native Livonians. Since peaceful conversion had not produce the desired results, Meinhard grew impatient and decided to convert the locals by force.

Initially, Meinhard's attempts to drum up military support failed miserably, and his plot went nowhere. Although he managed to attract a few soldiers and knights among the Saxons, many people refused to come. Instead, knights were far more interested in the defense of Jerusalem, which promised riches and the chance to join a developed institution of knighthood like the Templars or Hospitallers.

Meinhard died a failure in 1196, resulting in the arrival of a replacement in the guise of Bishop Berthold of Hanover, a Cistercian Abbot from Loccum. Berthold brought with him a massive contingent of crusaders intent on beating the pagans back, but he would not last long. He arrived in 1198 and was almost immediately killed in battle after deciding to ride ahead of his troops. The bishop was surrounded and executed by Livonians, after which the rest of the crusaders lost the upper hand and were slaughtered.

Back in Rome, Pope Innocent III grew frustrated. With two men having been killed at the hands of the Livonians, he ramped up his efforts for another crusade, issuing a formal papal bull declaring its beginning against the heretical Livonians. In exchange, he promised soldiers and knights their sins would be forgiven for eliminating the heretics. He also assigned a new leader for the area in the form of Bishop Albrecht von Buxthoeven. Buxthoeven was consecrated as bishop in 1199 and arrived in Livonia at the head of a new contingent of troops larger than the last, establishing Riga as the head of his bishopric in 1201. The following year, he formed the Livonian Brothers, officially beginning the organization in 1202, although its roots could be traced back two decades.

The Livonian Brothers experienced initial, rapid success, sparking rebellions among the Livonians. In response, the Germans tightened their grip on the region, smothering local trade. One of the Christened chiefs, Caupo, led the Livonians against the crusaders in repeated battles over the next three years, and while few records remain about the size of the opposing forces or territory gained or lost, the indigenous Livonians generally struggled against the crusaders. Caupo remained in charge until the Livonians were soundly defeated at Turaida in 1206, when the Christians hailed themselves as victors and the Livonians were made official converts.

In a surprise twist, Caupo accepted his defeat and became an ally of the crusaders until he died in 1217 during the Battle of St. Matthew's Day, which saw the Livonian Brothers and their local allies uniting to combat the counties of Estonia. In that battle, the crusaders sought to stem the tide of German regional control against approximately 6,000 soldiers. The Estonians lost, resulting in their mass baptism and the death of Chieftain Lembitu, one of their best leaders, who had tried to unite the Estonians under a single banner. His death further divided the region, which was great news for the Livonian Brothers, as they quickly took advantage of the splintered area to push German and Christian influence forward.

Fighting the Estonians

There was a decade between the Livonian conversion and the Battle of St. Matthew's Day, and the Swordbrothers used it to consolidate control over the region. By 1208, the Livonian Brothers captured notable Daugava trading posts and renamed them, resulting in the appearance of Holme, Kokenhusen, and Selburg in monastery records. Energetic campaigning also established new local alliances between the Latgalians, an ancient Baltic tribe in Eastern Latvia organized in a series of counties, and the crusaders. After they had allied with the Livonian Brothers, the knights constructed Cesis Castle and Koknese Castle, designed to replace the wooden Latgalian ones. Koknese was to be at the crux of the Daugavlda and Perse Rivers.

The ruins of Koknese Castle

The ruins of Cesis Castle

The Swordbrothers did not form alliances with all Latgalians. Several counties refused to surrender or make a deal, prompting the crusaders to target the nearby Principality of Jersika in 1209, and this situation led to the order's capture of the wife of Visvaldis, the ruler. Visvaldis loved his wife, but he also feared the order's power, so he submitted his kingdom to Bishop Buxthoeven, who merged the kingdom with the Archbishopric of Riga and granted part of it back to Visvaldis as a fief in exchange for loyalty to the Christians.

The other Latgalians faced more issues besides the Livonian Brothers. The Principality of Talava suffered considerably in wars against the Russians and Estonians. With little hope of remaining independent and wary of losing to their old enemies, Talava's nobles submitted to the crusaders, making it a vassal state of the Archbishopric of Riga around 1214. Talava was eventually divided between the Swordbrothersn and the Archbishopric, giving the Livonian Brothers a greater advantage in the region and putting them at odds with the Estonians, who still wanted the territory.

In the 13th century, the Estonians, one of the oldest Baltic tribes with centuries of infrastructure deeply entrenched in the region, were a major power in Eastern Europe, but by 1208, the crusaders believed they were powerful enough to begin significant operations against the Estonians, utilizing bases established in what was formerly Latgalian territory. At the time, the Estonians possessed eight major counties and seven smaller ones, led by regional elders, but these counties often did not cooperate and remained divided by local differences. They were, however, fierce in their defense against the Livonian Brothers when the crusaders mounted attacks into Sakala and Ugaunia in Southern Estonia. The raids were initially unsuccessful, and the Estonians brutally sacked Riga whenever possible.

As with the battles against the Latgalians and native Livonians, few detailed records remain about the conflict between the Swordbrothers and the Estonians, even though the war raged between 1208 and 1227. While the Livonian Brothers relied upon their vassal states for allies and some of the baptized local leaders, they had to contend with unfaithful allies, most notably the Livonians, Latgalians, and Russians forming the Republic of Novgorod, switching sides between the brotherhood and the Estonians with increasing frequency.

The Livonian Brothers concentrated on attacking Estonian hill forts that formed the centers of the Estonian counties (some historians and anthropologists have compared them to castles). The crusaders besieged the hill forts at every opportunity, resulting in an elaborate game in which the forts were captured, lost, and recaptured again and again until both sides grew weary of war. Eventually, the Swordbrothers entered a three-year truce with the Estonians, lasting from 1213-1215. During this time, the Germans, who formed the majority of the Livonian Brothers, consolidated their political position and stockpiled resources for the inevitable upcoming conflict. The Estonians, however, could not convince the counties to form a consolidated state, no matter how temporary the arrangement.

When the truce ended in 1215, the Swordbrothers had the advantage, and while the crusaders hoped to spread Christianity and eliminate heretics, the knights were more interested in preserving Saxon power in the region and keeping profitable trade routes open because they benefitted from the trade. In addition to bolstering their coffers and those of the Church, their successes acquired more territory in which Christians could settle. Estonia possessed its own allure, with land that could be used to develop new trade routes, so the Swordbrothers began the war against the Estonians, led by Lembitu of Lehola, anew. Lembitu, the elder and leader of Sackalia, the center of Estonian resistance, kept the Estonians strong for six years until the fateful Battle of St. Matthew's Day on September 21, 1217, in which he perished.

A year later, the Livonian Brothers faced new competition from other Christian kingdoms who wanted a piece of Eastern Europe. Denmark and Sweden arrived, eager to expand the eastern coast of the Baltic Sea, and when their forces showed up in 1218, Buxthoeven asked for assistance from King Valdemar II of Denmark. Instead, Valdemar made a deal with the Livonian Brothers, pitting the Church against the rising religious knighthood, which meant the order would need to share its spoils from the war against the Estonians if any were won.

Valdemar II earned some fast victories, including at the Battle of Lindanise in Revelia around the year 1219. Many historians speculate the battle helped to create the design of the current Flag of Denmark. He also founded Castrum Danorum, an influential fortress that survived two sieges by the Estonians in 1220 and 1223.

A modern picture of Castrum Danorum

Meanwhile, King John I of Sweden attempted to establish a presence in the area by attacking the county of Wiek, but his troops were assaulted and defeated by local Oeselians in the Battle of Lihula around 1220. With Sweden gone, the Swordbrothers and the Danes leaped upon the rest of northern Estonia, claiming Harrien, Revelia, and Virumaa over the next three years.

The war would worsen and grow more brutal as the conflict for Estonia came to a head between 1223 and 1224. The Livonian Brothers, along with their allies, lost all Christian strongholds in the region except for one, and all of the defenders were slaughtered. The Estonian victory would not last, however; in 1224, the crusaders doubled their efforts and took back all of the larger fortresses except Tharbata, which was manned by 200 Russian mercenaries and an angry and determined garrison of Estonian natives who refused to fall to the crusaders' siege. The leader of the Russian mercenaries was an enterprising man named Vyachko, and he had been told he could have the fortress and its nearby land "if he could conquer them for himself."[3] He never got the chance to keep it, as the crusaders returned in late summer to capture the fortress and kill the surviving defenders, including Vyachko.

After the taking of Tharbata, Holy Roman Emperor Frederick II announced that Livonia, Prussia, Sambia, and some of the neighboring provinces around the Baltic Sea would be considered *reichsfrei*. Thus, instead of being under the control of local rulers, the officials governing these lands would be subordinates of the Holy Roman Empire and the Catholic Church. Shortly afterward, Pope Honorius III appointed Bishop William of Modena as the papal legate for the region, sending a new priest to be intermediary between the *reichsfrei* and the Church.

---

[3] Arbusow 1982: 246

Wolfgang Rieger's picture of a contemporary statue of Emperor Frederick II

Little changed for the Livonian Brothers despite the switch in management. The knights of the order were still called upon to defend trade routes and take new territory, and many of the soldiers were deeply embedded in the tricky business of keeping Estonian locals subordinate while politicians and popes hundreds of miles away played power politics. To simplify matters, the Livonian Brothers established a new headquarters at Fellin in Sackalia and founded several more defensible strongholds like Wenden, Segewold, and Ascheraden. Knights and clerics could move between the fortresses as needed to maintain the borders of the Christian territories, though frequent raids by displaced Estonians and other peoples were common. Pilgrimages to Eastern Europe picked up around 1224 and 1225, meaning Christians from Western Europe came to see relics and visit churches.

Fighting Saaremaa

The final major conflict for the Livonian Brothers was their ongoing war against Saaremaa, the last Estonian county managing to evade conquest by being a remote island nation possessing war fleets capable of raiding coastal fortresses. Saaremaa sent vessels to pillage Denmark and

Sweden even while battling Saxon crusaders, returning with loot and resources to aid in the war effort. This formidable enemy kept the Swordbrothers on their toes for over 60 years.

The Livonian Brothers' first attack took place in 1216 when the crusaders allied with local Bishop Theodorich's personal guard. Together, they marched to Saaremaa across the frozen sea, separating the island from the mainland, and pillaged the coastline and nearby towns before heading back across the icy water. To retaliate, the nearby Oeselians decimated German-held territories throughout Latvia in the following spring.

In 1220, King John I of Sweden joined forces with Bishop Karl of Linköping to take several fortresses in Western Estonia in an effort to break resistance. The Oeselians, however, would not be beaten, and they attacked the Swedish stronghold of Lihula, killing the entire garrison as well as the Bishop.

Frustrated with the situation in Eastern Europe, Danish King Valdemar II attempted another conquest of Saaremaa, and he enlisted the Livonian Brotherhood's help. They established a stone fortress and created a new garrison, but it was besieged and lost within five days. The Danish garrison returned to nearby Revel, leaving Bishop Albert of Riga's brother behind as a hostage. The Oeselians leveled the castle to prevent future insurgencies, but that effort proved futile.[4]

In 1227, the Livonian Brothers teamed up with Riga's soldiers to launch a combined attack against Saaremaa. They destroyed the Muhu and Valjala strongholds, leaving the Oeselians without a leg on which to stand. With nowhere to retreat, the Oeselians officially accepted Christianity, though they continued to practice their beliefs and religion when the crusaders were not around.

The conflict was still far from over, and Saaremaa continued to be a hotbed of activity. Skirmishes continued for the next nine years, culminating in the brutal defeat of the Livonian Brothers at the Battle of Saule in 1236. The defeat served to spawn intensified warfare with Saaremaa.

This bout of fighting culminated with the Oeselians being forced to accept Christianity once more in 1241. The Oeselians signed treaties with the grandmaster of the Livonian Order, Andreas de Velven, as well as the local Bishopric of Osel-Wiek. Another treaty was written and signed in 1255, this time by Grandmaster Anno Sangerhausenn and the Oeselian elders, who had their names phonetically transcribed by local Latin monks. The treaty officially kept the Oeselians under the control of the Catholic Church but granted the people rights regarding land ownership and inheritance, social structure, and religious practice.

---

[4] Urban 1994

A surviving copy of the treaty

The conflict was still not over, however. While the Livonian Brothers spent the next six years fortifying their position in Eastern Europe, the Oeselians bolstered their ranks, and in 1261, they slaughtered the Germans on the island and renounced Christianity. Another peace treaty was brokered when the Oeselians were soundly defeated by an army consisting of the Livonian Brothers, Danish Estonia, and soldiers from the Bishopric of Osel-Wiek. In the wake of this fighting, the Livonian Brothers built another stone fort for protection, this time at Pöide.

Peace was maintained over the next 80 years, but war broke out yet again on July 24, 1343. The Oeselians rose up once more to slaughter all of the Germans on Saaremaa, drown the clerics, and besiege the Livonian Brothers' fortress at Pöide. The garrison was forced to surrender, and the Livonian Brothers were herded out and massacred before the fort was burned to the ground. In retaliation, Burchard von Dreileben led a campaign across the frozen sea in February 1344 to find the Oeselians' stronghold. The Germans defeated the Oeselians, hanged their leader, and made Saaremaa a Livonian Brothers vassal state, a status it would formally retain until 1559.

Fighting the Semigallians

Much information about the Semigallians' encounters with the Swordbrothers comes from the *Livonian Chronicle of Henry*, a contemporary narrative outlining the history of Livonia that was likely meant to serve as a report for William of Modena. According to the document, the Semigallians formed an alliance against the Livonians with the Bishop of Riga, who had rebelled around 1203. In exchange, the Bishopric of Riga supplied military support to the Semigallians to help them beat back Lithuanian attacks in 1205. In 1207, the Semigallians also aided Caupo, the christened Livonian chief, to take his castle back from nearby pagan rebels.

In 1219, the Livonian Brothers managed to annul the alliance by invading Semigallia despite the treaties of peace and assistance, and in response, the Semigallians created an alliance with the nearby Curonians and Lithuanians. After years of sporadic battles, the Semigallians and Curonians attacked the Daugaygrica Monastery, the primary crusader stronghold in the region, along the Daugava River Delta in 1228, displacing the Livonian Brothers. As revenge, the crusaders invaded Semigallia, resulting in Semigallians pillaging nearby land.[5]

Warfare continued for the next 42 years, ending in a bloody standstill in which the crusaders and Semigallians slaughtered one another over the same territory while frequently crossing the frozen Gulf of Riga to do so. At one point in 1270, the Livonian Brothers were soundly defeated and the grandmaster was killed following a siege of Livonia. Grand Duke Traidenis of Lithuania decided to aid the Semigallians in their war, setting off an all-out decimation by the 1280s that resulted in the crusaders burning fields and causing famine. In response, 100,000 locals migrated to Lithuania to continue the fight against the Germans, and the unconquered regions of Semigallia and Curonia unified under the rule of the Grand Duchy of Lithuania, forcing the Livonian Brothers to face a more cohesive foe.

There would be no satisfying conclusion for the Livonian Brothers. Instead of achieving victory, they were forced to merge with the Teutonic Order of Prussia to create the Livonian Order. Afterward, the order tried to exert its influence and became known as an arm of the Teutonic Knights, whom history remembers well. They would never truly control Eastern Europe, and tensions between the Christians and native populations would continue for centuries after the initial Livonian Crusade.

---

[5] Urban 1994

A map of the region in 1260

The Fall of the Teutonic Knights

By the time the Livonian Brothers had merged with the Teutonic Knights, the Teutonic Knights had crushed, conquered, and now held reign over 5 of the 7 principal Prussian regions, such as Bartia, Warmia, Pomesania, Poegesania, and Natangia, spawning what collectively came to be called the "Monastic State of the Teutonic Order." Pope Gregory IX's *Golden Bull of Rieti* confirmed the order's possession over the newly risen crusader state, and allowed it to do as it wished so long as it paid its respects to the pope. About 7 years into the Prussian conquest, membership experienced another jump when the order brought into the fold the Livonian Brothers of the Sword (or the Livonian Sword Brethren), a military-religious brotherhood founded by the Bishop of Riga, as well as the Polish-born Order of Dobrzyn, making the organizations a part of its entity.

To combat Prussia's population problem, which was in danger of dying out due to revolts, invasions, and the evils of the plague, the knights decided to furnish the place with new colonists, just as they had in Burzenland. As they continued to address the pagan issue, shiploads of Catholic colonists from Belgium, Poland, Germany, the Netherlands, and other lands of the Holy Roman Empire spilled onto the Prussian shore. The knights wasted no time in reaching out to the colonists for their help in establishing castles and forts to secure their new plots of conquered land.

The order's controversial conversion tactics were as savage as they were black and white. A Prussian captive's baptism was their only hope of release and maintaining some sort of normalcy in their life under the stifling Teutonic reign. Those who so much as protested were either put down or forever banished from their homelands. This was not to say the Prussians accepted their new fates; on the contrary, the boldest of the bunch who refused to lose their culture squared off against the knights, with quite a few succeeding in "roasting captured brethren alive in their armor, like chestnuts, before the shrine of a local god."

Uprisings became unavoidable in this feral and treacherous climate, and during its Prussian reign, a total of 5 full-fledged insurgencies threatened to topple everything the knights had built thus far. The second revolt, now remembered as the infamous "Great Prussian Uprising" of 1260, was the largest and most severe of its kind, claiming the most Teutonic casualties. At least 150 knights allegedly perished in a single session, a sobering figure that only paled in comparison to the unknown number of lives lost to the Teutonic sword in the 13th century. By the time the last uprising in 1295 had wound down, the German language had become the official language in what was now a mainly Christian Prussia.

Mariusz Kędzierski's picture of the ruins of the Teutonic castle in Rehden, one of five castles not captured by the Prussians

The fast-paced growth of the monastic state might have been applauded by the papacy and most European Christians, but many did not hesitate to shine a light on the knights' unorthodox military techniques and callous treatment of the pagan Prussians. These naysayers accused the knights of taking the Lord's word out of context to justify all the bloodshed and heartache they caused. One of the most vocal critics of the time was the celebrated English philosopher, Roger Bacon, who chose to use his platform to raise awareness of the order's misdeeds in 1266. Said Bacon, "[T]he brothers of the Teutonic Order much disturb the conversion of infidels because of the wars which they are always starting, and because of the fact that they wish to dominate them absolutely...The pagan race has many times been ready to receive the faith in peace after preaching, but those of the Teutonic order do not wish to allow this, because they wish to subjugate them and reduce them to slavery." Women and children were not spared either, since the order perceived them as little more than human, and as such, "not worthy of life."

By the mid-13th century, as the Livonian Brothers were struggling, the superiors of the Teutonic Order had already been briefed about the weakened state of Russia, and they, too, wanted in on what they saw as a territorial free-for-all. Their plans were met with the enthusiastic support of Pope Gregory IX, who encouraged the knights to set forth and "Christianize" Russia. In 1240, a Teutonic-sponsored army of German, Danish, and Estonian knights, ex-Livonian Sword Brethren, and Russian renegades burst into the city of Pskov and held it hostage. There, they captured the Bjorg Castle and effortlessly vanquished its inhabitants. Thrilled with the cakewalk of a victory, they left behind only 50 attendants and 2 knights to hold down the new fort.

A Renaissance depiction of Pope Gregory IX

Alexander Nevsky, the 20-something Prince of Novgorod, was appalled by the nerve of the Christian attackers, and decided to nip the Teutonic problem in the bud before it could spread. Nevsky countered the knights' forces with his own band of Russian warriors and mercenaries, slaying any Estonian knight or Russian traitor that he came across, and setting their prisoners free. He then headed for Pskov and surrounded the Bjorg Castle, causing the startled knights and attendants to stumble over one another as they scurried away from the scene. Finally, in April 1242, the Teutonic knights were trounced by Nevsky's men in what is now memorialized as the "Massacre on the Ice," the fateful battle occurring between Lakes Pskov and Peipus.

The Christian cause fared no better in the latter half of the 13th century. Between April and May of 1291, the Muslim Mamluks of Egypt laid siege to the coveted city of Acre once more. The defining moment came when the Mamluk leader, Sultan Al-Ashraf Khalil, led his men into the city on the 18th of May. Here, they proceeded to occupy all of Acre's buildings, save for the Templar stronghold, and lopped off villagers' heads left and right. The Christians did what they could to keep the Mamluks at bay, but they could only manage to hold out for another 10 days before they could hold on no longer. And with that, the Muslims broke into the last crusader stronghold, and went to work uprooting the foundations of the Latin kingdom of Jerusalem.

With Acre now under Muslim dominion, the order was left with no other alternative but to shut the doors of its headquarters. They relocated to Cyprus for some time, before finding more permanent lodgings in Venice at the Santa Trinità, which served as their new base for the next 18 years. There, they plotted the recapture of the Crusader States, sharpened their recruiting tactics, and mustered a humble army of Italian knights, seemingly retiring their Germans-only policy in this time of crisis.

It was also here that the knights began to contemplate a new venture. The knights were still feeling the fresh burns of their recent defeats, but they were determined to see them as nothing more than mere hiccups. At this point, they did not have much more to lose, but they had everything to gain. And so, the order turned its attention towards an untouched region of the pagan Baltic – Prussian Lithuania.

The order, along with chivalric brotherhoods from France, England, and other neighboring Christian European countries, began by embarking on *reyse* runs, or in English, "seasonal campaigns." Most of these runs, which consisted of about 100 men a time, were orchestrated by thrill-seeking religious justice warriors who sought out to play their part in the evangelization of the infidels without having to make the arduous journey to the Middle East. Armed with spears, crossbows, swords, and other intimidating weapons, it did not take long for Lithuanian residents to surrender to the Christian knights. Apart from violence and pillaging, the knights raped and tortured its residents into submission. Surviving women were then used as sex toys, and the men for free manual labor.

The order would not take their conquest of Lithuania seriously until 1337, when Emperor Louis IV presented the order with a charter that granted them the authority to capture all of Lithuania and Russia. In late January of 1348, troops led by the soon-to-be *Hochmeister* Winrich von Kniprode crashed the towns and cities of central Lithuania, such as Vitebsk, Polotsk, Volodymyr-Volynskyi, and Smolensk, among others. Lithuanian defenders attempted to put up a fight, but were ultimately overpowered by the knights on a battle upon the frozen Strėva River. For the knights, things only got better from there, as they moved forward with little to no resistance at all. They tore apart one of the most prestigious castles in Veliuona, ransacked the city of Šiauliai, and continued to pitch up their flags and banners in Smolensk, Pskov, and Novgorod in 1349.

Just 21 years later, the Grand Duchy of Lithuania suffered yet another crippling loss at the Battle of Rudau. Some sources claimed that up to 5,500 Lithuanian men lost their lives on the field, but many historians today believe these figures have been embellished for dramatic effect. To commemorate their win at Rudau, the knights built an Augustinian convent at Heiligenbeli in honor of the Blessed Virgin Mary.

By the early years of the 15th century, the order now bore strongholds in Pomerelia, Samogitia, Prussia, Livonia, Estonia, Courland, Gotland, Neumark, Ösel, and Dagö. It appeared as if there was no hope of hampering the powerful strides of the ever-growing monastic state. Little did the knights know, they were about to meet their match.

In 1386, the Grand Duke of Lithuania was dunked into the local river and baptized into Christianity with an extravagant ceremony. He then married the Polish Queen Jadwiga of Poland, and by right, was crowned King Jogaila of Poland. This only strengthened the budding bond between the 2 territories, their combined efforts now a threat looming over the order's heads.

Now that Prussia and Lithuania had been thoroughly "Christianized," the Christians' primary mission was technically accomplished, but the newfound friendship between Poland and Lithuania did not sit well with the order. Rather than consider this a job well done and move on to their next venture, the knights called the Jogaila's conversion a scam and accused the Polish crown of secretly fraternizing with enemy infidels.

It was not the order's first brush with Poland, which, in hindsight, could have been why the order was so affected by the Polish-Lithuanian union. Back in 1308, the Kingdom of Poland hired the Teutonic knights to capture what was then the Prussian city of Danzig, and to extinguish the uprisings against the Polish sovereign there. The knights did as they were instructed and seized the city's main fortress, but when it came time to pay up, the Polish king stiffed them, leaving them hanging with the tab for their services unpaid. Many say this was the event that led to the falling out between them.

In 1409, a rebellion erupted in Samogitia, one of the order's possessions in Lithuania. The knights, who were already irritated by the less-than-pleasant news, grew even more exasperated when they heard that the Duke Vytautas of Lithuania was one of the most ardent supporters of the cause. The Teutonic *Hochmeister* at the time, Ulrich von Jungingen, ordered the Duke to withdraw his support and persuade the rebels to stop their nonsense at once – if he failed to do so, the knights were coming to finish the job themselves.

Lithuanian authorities were mortally offended by Jungingen's brash ultimatums, so, instead of backing down, they called upon their new Polish buddies for aid. Jungingen did not take this lightly, and on the 6th of August, he declared war on both Lithuania and Poland. The 3 parties battled on for 2 months until they reached a truce, segueing into a period of peace that lasted a little under a year. By June of 1410, whatever compromise the quarreling parties reached was balled up in their fists and tossed out the windows.

The knights prepared themselves for 2 separate attacks, but unbeknownst to them, the Polish and Lithuanian forces had decided to sneak across the border of Marienburg, where the knights were stationed, and launch a joint ambush on the order there. On July 9, 1410, that was exactly what the joint forces did. The knights soldiered on until the very end, and made a Hail Mary attempt at a final defense at their base by Grunwald, which soon proved to be a fruitless endeavor. The knights were annihilated, and the few who survived were either imprisoned or fled for their lives without once glancing over their shoulders. At least 14,000 knights were captured and imprisoned. Approximately 8,000 of them were said to have perished, among them Grand Master Jungingen and other high-ranking officials of the order.

A depiction of the Battle of Grunwald

On February 1, 1411, all 3 parties ended their squabbles with the Peace of Thorn. The terms of the treaty have been dissected repeatedly by historians ever since, with many believing that the Polish-Lithuanian side, though the victors, had lost out on the deal. Samogitia was returned to the jurisdiction of King Jogaila and Duke Vytautas, but this expired upon the rulers' deaths. This was a condition the knights tolerated with ease, for both Jogaila and Vytautas were far from spring chickens. The order was also made to relinquish its claim on Dobrzyn, which was handed back to Poland. In exchange, the Polish and Lithuanian rulers promised to convert the remaining pagans in Samogitia and Lithuania.

The loss of the 2 territories had barely put a dent in the order's armor, but it would be the ransom payment agreement in the treaty's terms that marked the beginning of the end for them. Most of the 14,000 captives were released not long after the Grunwald atrocities, but those who remained – many of them the biggest names in the order – were made to pay colossal fines in return for their freedom. To make matters more palatable for the Polish-Lithuanian parties, the treaty required the order to pay all the captives' ransoms in one lump sum – 100,000 kopas. This was equivalent to roughly 44,000 lb of silver; they could also choose to pay portions of the bill in 4 yearly installments. If the order failed to cough up what was owed at any given time, the price would be jacked up to 720,000 kopas, which was estimated to have been 10 times the salary of the King of England.

The order scrabbled to find ways to cover their debt in the hopes of dodging their impending doom. With their tails between their legs, they sought financial aid from abroad and raised taxes in Danzig and Thorn, which was met by more revolts and resistance. They paddled hard, and for some time, managed to stay afloat, and met the deadlines for the first 2 installments. But by the third installment, authorities ran out of fingers to plug in the holes sprouting all over the ship. The order's funds were almost completely drained from having to keep up with paychecks, repair costs, lavish gifts to keep up appearances and relations, and whatnot. The ship was sinking fast.

The treaty clearly specified that any territorial disputes from there on out would be rectified through civil international relations, but perhaps unsurprisingly, it was only a matter of time before one of the parties went back on their word. In the early 1450s, Prussians began to rise up against what they viewed as their tyrannical oppressors, and revolted against the knights. This kicked off the Thirteen Years' War, which pitted the State of the Teutonic Order against an alliance between the Prussian Confederation and the Polish kingdom.

Following the order's humbling defeat, a Second Peace of Thorn was drawn up with Pope Paul II as the mediator on October 10, 1466. The order was forced to hand over the lands of Danzig, Pomerelia, Culmerland, Warmia, Allenstein, and Marienburg, most of which were ceded to the Polish Crown, a province that soon became known as "Royal Prussia." From that day forward, Royal Prussia belonged solely to the Polish kingdom. At this juncture, the order was left with only a handful of territories in Eastern Prussia. Even then, the treaty made it clear that its residents would kowtow only to the Polish king, and the *Hochmeister*'s role was reduced to nothing more than the "Senator of the Polish Kingdom."

In a twist only few in the order could have seen coming, after the last Polish-Teutonic War, which ended in 1521, *Hochmeister* Albert of Brandenburg was befriended by the one and only Martin Luther. Luther was said to have talked him into abandoning the order's traditions and urged him to take a bride to keep the brotherhood from losing any more steam in Prussia. 4 years later, Albert shocked his peers by announcing his decision to convert to Lutheranism. With no leg left to stand on, the Teutonic Order was squeezed out of the region, including Prussia, altogether.

Martin Luther

The brotherhood was never able to truly recuperate from the barrage of setbacks thrown their way, and in the following centuries, the order continued to deteriorate. By the 19th century, only parts of the Teutonic bailiwicks in Austria and Tyrol remained. In 1810, Napoleon would have a field day with the order's properties in Mergentheim, and within a few years, the Teutonic Order was officially adopted by the Habsburgs of the Austrian Empire. In 1929, the Austrian wing of the Teutonic Order was stripped of its knightly and military duties, and declared nothing more but a clerical order within the Roman Catholic Church.

The Livonian Chronicle of Henry

One of the best cultural sources for the Livonian Brothers is the aforementioned Latin document that described the fighting throughout Livonia from 1180-1227. Known as *The Livonian Chronicle of Henry*, it was written by a priest named Henry of Latvia and inscribed circa 1229, and many historians consider the document to be the oldest written document about the history of Livonia. *The Livonian Chronicle of Henry* is one of the only surviving pieces of evidence from which historians can reconstruct battles and altercations between the peoples of the eastern Baltic and the Christian missionaries and crusaders. Many historians have relied on

The Livonian Chronicle of Henry along with the *Livonian Rhymed Chronicle* and the *Novgorod First Chronicle* to explain the complexities of crusading ideology and the political and economic benefits sought by the Livonian Brothers and other missionaries throughout the region. For example, the documents note that merchants were common on the front lines and among the knights, indicating the economic benefits of attempting to convert the Baltic peoples. At the same time, historians are hesitant to rely on the documents to understand native Baltic peoples because the sources are inherently biased.

The Livonian Chronicle of Henry reveals significant information not only about the Livonian Brothers but of other unaffiliated knights who joined the Livonian Crusade without seeking membership in the order. The document noted that "the crusader[s] in this area, unlike the crusaders in the [h]oly [l]and, [were] held to a chronologically defined term[s] of service."[6] This term typically lasted a year, meaning that the knights were held to fewer religious and political obligations and did not need to uphold the same tenets or laws as their counterparts in the Middle East or around the Mediterranean Sea. The document also places the thrust of the Livonian Crusade squarely on the shoulders of Bishop Albert, not the papacy, which would have been standard for other undertakings.

As far as scholars can tell, the document was written by a monk in the first generation of conversion in Livonia after Bishop Albert of Buxhoeveden took over. Once he had gained authority over the land, the Livonian Brothers managed to conquer more and more territory, leading to one individual inscribing *The Livonian Chronicle of Henry*. Besides pertinent information about the order, the document also reveals the opinionated, cruel, and often demeaning rhetoric used by crusaders to describe native pagans, as well as Livonian duplicity. For example, the crusaders knew pagans would not convert in exchange for forts or trade (even though the native Livonians accepted the deal), so they concluded that force was the sole option.[7]

Another interesting fact pulled from the document is the confusion many in the order felt about their role in the Crusades. While those that went to take and protect Jerusalem had a clear goal in mind and strong historical and religious ties to their location, the same could not be said for those who went to Livonia. Once the native Livonians had been suppressed and conquered, the Bishop of Riga continued to send them forward, but with no clear-cut goal in mind, many knights became disillusioned and restless.

Perhaps the most important role of *The Livonian Chronicle of Henry* is not how it provides eyewitness accounts of the Livonian Crusade, but how it gives modern historians a peek into murky history. The document provides insight into military operations, the complexities of religious motives, and Church officials' political aims for the Crusades, as well as details about the local culture and how the knights acted out. It also explains how many of the knights justified

---

[6] Brundage 1983:4
[7] Lettus 2004

their presence, often by claiming that the conquest of Livonia was in the name of the Virgin Mary and that the region was the Land of the Virgin Mary. This perception began after Bishop Meinhard established a Cult of Mary convent in the region; the cult continued under successive Bishops of Riga, including Albert, who named the Episcopal Church in Livonia the Church of the Virgin Mary, in the early 1200s.

Besides this religious justification, *The Livonian Chronicle of Henry* makes it clear that the majority of the knights and soldiers present sought absolution of sins. Some individuals were cold-blooded killers who were tired of the tension between German Christians and patrons, while others sought wealth and fame along trade routes.

The Structure of the Order

The Livonian Brothers resembled many other religious knighthoods spawned in the Middle Ages, including a clear division between monks and knights. Although both were required to take religious vows, the monks focused on administrative and theological aspects of the order while the knights were tasked with defending pilgrims, beating back pagans, and taking new territory for Christianity.

The order's membership consisted of different ranks of men and banned women in an effort to preserve the fraternity of the organization and prevent the monks and knights from leaving illegitimate children behind. Members were divided between brother knights, priests, and clerks, as well as lay brothers, and they were assisted in their day-to-day affairs by non-members like mercenaries, local domestic servants, and esquires. Additionally, some sections of the order kept indentured servants or slaves who were considered domestic help, ranging from *halpbruderen* to *slaven*.[8] These servants and slaves were taken from the local population.

Brother knights - military officials forced to take vows of poverty and celibacy - held the most power in the Livonian Brothers despite the fact the organization was nominally controlled by the Catholic Church. Brother knights were responsible for the election of the grand commander, who controlled the institution and everyone in it, and brother knights worked with local religious leaders, especially Bishop Albert, who was responsible for beginning the Livonian Crusade.

All members of the Livonian Brothers were aware of some inherent disparities in the organization's structure. For example, while the knights were supposed to be religious and adhere to their vows, such rules were rarely followed in practice because the clergy had to catch a lay brothers' bad behavior before he could punish him. The Church did, however, still hold some influence, especially among priests responsible for ensuring knights received supplies necessary to continue their work.

The Rule of the Livonian Brothers of the Sword described the role of the priests as being "a

---

[8] Sterns 1982:84-111

worthy and useful role, for in time of peace they shine in the midst of the lay brethren, urge them to observe strictly the rules, celebrate for them divine service, and administer to them the sacraments… [and in war] strengthen the brethren for battle and admonish them to remember how God also suffered death for them on the Cross."[9] However, these priests were vastly outnumbered by the knights and only exerted their influence in urban centers less likely to be attacked by native Baltic peoples, like Riga. Despite this lowly position, the clerics were still better off than the male and female slaves taken by the order and forced into servitude, both sexual and domestic.

The Influence of the Knights in Nationalism and Popular Culture

As is the case with many other religious knighthoods, the illustrious reputation of the Teutonic Order faded fast in the 20th century when Emperor Wilhelm II of Germany posed for a picture wearing the traditional garb of a Teutonic monk. The photograph, depicting the emperor climbing up the stairs of Marienburg Castle, would quickly become a symbol of German imperial policy throughout the country. The Teutonic Order would suffer further when famous German historians like Heinrich von Treitschke used Teutonic Knight imagery to promote pro-German nationalist and anti-Polish rhetoric. The imagery and symbols were also adopted by a suffering German middle-class, seeking scapegoats behind the economic upheaval and depression following World War I that plagued the Weimar Republic. This recession saw the rise of nationalistic associations and organizations, as well as the growth of racism and imperialism. All of this helped lay the groundwork for Nazi Germany.

Teutonic Knight imagery and symbolism became a part of Nazi propaganda before and during World War II. Many Nazis tried to depict the knights' actions in Eastern Europe as a precursor to Nazi conquests in the search of *Lebensraum*, or living space, for the German people. Instead of converting heretics to Christianity, the focus was on ethnic cleansing, so only the pure and strong would remain. Heinrich Himmler notably attempted to describe the SS as the reincarnation of the Teutonic Knights, even as, in a twisted turn of events, the order was banned in 1938 and members were persecuted by the Nazis due to the religious nature of the organization.

One of the best examples of Teutonic Knight imagery used to bolster Nazi Germany as propaganda came from a painting commissioned and chosen by Adolf Hitler in 1935. The image, called "Der Bannerträger" ("The Standard Bearer"), features Hitler holding a Nazi flag and dressed in medieval plate mail, and it was copied in the late 1930s, printed on postcards, and used to promote nationalism and the Nazi regime. The painting, which was stabbed by a U.S. soldier upon discovery, is currently in the Holocaust Memorial Museum in Washington, D.C.

---

[9] Sterns 1982:85

At the same time, Polish nationalists resisted the Germans by conflating Teutonic Knight imagery with the Nazis and Germans in general. Soviet propagandists also picked up on the trend, and individuals in Western Europe soon began to associate Nazi Germany with the Teutonic Knights.

Given their connection with the Teutonic Knights and the fact the Livonian Brothers of the Sword left indelible marks upon the fabric of European history, it's ironic that the order is largely forgotten when the Crusades are discussed. Regardless, the Livonian Brothers paved for the way for the development of a wealthier Holy Roman Empire, and they greatly bolstered the more famous Teutonic Knights. Along with them, the Livonian Brothers would help unify various peoples and nations in Eastern Europe, leaving a lasting legacy that would be seized upon for different reasons by multiple nations on all sides of World War II.

Online Resources

Other books about Catholic history by Charles River Editors

Other books about the Livonian Brothers of the Sword on Amazon

Bibliography

Arbusow, L., & Bauer, A. (1982). *Heinrici Chronicon Livoniae = Livländische Chronik* (E. Tarvel, Ed.). Tallinn: Eesi Raamat.

Asbridge, T. (2011). *The Crusades: The Authoritative History of the War for the Holy Land*. New York: Ecco *Press*.

Brundage, J. A., Urban, W., & Boockmann, H. (1983). The Livonian Crusade. *The American Historical Review*,88(1), 96. doi:10.2307/1869376

Lettus, Henricus. (2004). *The Chronicle of Henry of Livonia*. New York, NY: Columbia University Press.

Pluskowski, A. (2013). *The Archaeology of the Prussian Crusade: Holy War and Colonisation*. London: Routledge.

Selart, Anti., & Robb, F. (2015). *Livonia, Rus and the Baltic Crusades in the Thirteenth Century*. Leiden, Netherlands: Brill.

Seward, Desmond. (1995). *The Monks of War: The Military Religious Orders*. London: Penguin Books.

Sterns, Indrikis. (1982). Crime and Punishment among the Teutonic Knights. *Speculum*,57(1), 84-111. doi:10.2307/2847563

Urban, William L. (1994). *The Baltic Crusade*. Chicago, IL: Lithuanian Research and Studies Center.

Urban, William L. (2018). *The Last Years of the Teutonic Knights: Lithuania, Poland, and the Teutonic Order*. Barnsley, S. Yorkshire: Greenhill Books.

Urban, William. L. (2003). *The Teutonic Knights: A Military History*. London: Greenhill Books.

Voltaire, François-Marie Arouet. (1756) "Essay on Customs."

Free Books by Charles River Editors

We have brand new titles available for free most days of the week. To see which of our titles are currently free, click on this link.

Discounted Books by Charles River Editors

We have titles at a discount price of just 99 cents everyday. To see which of our titles are currently 99 cents, click on this link.

CPSIA information can be obtained
at www.ICGtesting.com
Printed in the USA
LVHW061431130720
660544LV00033B/1924